Get Positive Revolution

Words to Live By

K.J. ENOKA

BALBOA.
PRESS

A DIVISION OF HAY HOUSE

Balboa Press books may be ordered through booksellers or by contacting:

Balboa Press
A Division of Hay House
1663 Liberty Drive
Bloomington, IN 47403
www.balboapress.com.au
1-(877) 407-4847

ISBN: 978-1-4525-1169-6 (sc)
ISBN: 978-1-4525-1170-2 (e)

Printed in the United States of America

Balboa Press rev. date: 11/20/2013

Dedication

This book was inspired by my beautiful sister Kerry who gave me insight into the magic we all possess that is, **the power of thought**, and inspiration to use that magic to help others realise that positive change begins with the words we speak and the thoughts we choose.

Thank you my beautiful sister. You are blissfully unaware of your positive influence and the wonderful world you exposed me to. How grateful I am to have you in my life. I love you as only a sister can.

xxx

Acknowledgement

I acknowledge my family and friends for your endless support and love and the following authors whose teachings have inspired and encouraged me to be creative and follow my dreams. Louise Hay, Esther and Jerry Hicks, Eckhart Tolle, Dr Wayne Dyer. I have connected with so many through this journey and thank you all for your valuable contribution to this book.

It doesn't matter if you start the journey
alone...the ones who are meant to
join you will catch up

Having an abundance of anything is nothing if not shared to help enhance the lives of others. Let your intention be to give....not just receive

Knowing what you want and where you want to be is one thing. Allowing it into your life is another. Open your eyes and your heart to the magnificence that is YOU and allow the journey to begin

Plant kindness, grow love ♡

Step up and shine before someone else steals the show

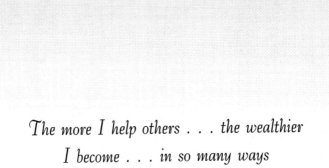

The more I help others . . . the wealthier I become . . . in so many ways

A grateful heart will prosper

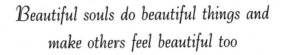

Beautiful souls do beautiful things and make others feel beautiful too

If it's not serving you in a positive way . . .
it's not growing you in a positive way

*The one with a generous heart
is a rich person indeed*

It's not bad luck or a mistake or even an accident that things happen the way they do. It's called choices and we all make them. Thoughts produce choices and every choice has an outcome

If you want to get happy . . . .

think happy thoughts ☺

Replenish your heart with a smile.
The most powerful weapon in
the face of anger

Failure is simply a sign you need to try a different approach.
Remember....success comes from failure!

The more you worry about what others think, the more unhappy you'll be. Please yourself . . . not the rest of the world

If there's no joy and love in the company you're keeping . . . you're probably keeping the wrong company

Peace + Love = Happy ☺

Use your time wisely. You are here
to transform and enhance the lives of
others through love and kindness. Create
opportunities to help others see their purpose
so we may all enjoy a peaceful, tranquil,
happy earth and all it has to offer

If things don't go to plan . . . . it's only because the universe has other plans in store. Trust that all will be as it should be

Your past doesn't determine
your future . . . . Your choices do

Contribute to your own life and the lives of others in a way that inspires and empowers

Step into each new day only allowing thoughts that consistently improve the way you feel

Sometimes I catch myself feeling uneasy about where I sit. Then I remember . . . . I can change it. I have the power to open and close doors and choose another path

Being in a place that makes you feel uncomfortable brings about a decision that will inspire you to be in a place that feels better. Don't settle for anything less than you deserve

Your lack of anything is due only to the
thoughts you offer. Stand in a place that
feels good and allow your desires
to unfold before you

Be driven by your passion. Passion inspires determination, determination motivates success

I choose 'HAPPY' because HAPPY FEELS GOOD!

Go away Self Doubt; I'm too busy having fun with my new found confidence!

Kindness is so good for the heart

*Raise your ability to connect with
the things you want.
THINK good!
FEEL good!
GET good!*

Don't expect any good to come from an
act of revenge. The negative intent you
project on another will most certainly have
a boomerang effect. Remember . . .
what you give is what you get!

Your happiness is not dependent on me . . . .
just as my happiness is not
dependent on you

Everything before me is a result of MY thinking not yours

Your strong desire to have stimulates creation and brings forth the very thing you've been thinking about

When your heart is filled with love and
kindness and you want to share it with
others . . . . that's what makes
you truly beautiful

Tell yourself you're GOOD ENOUGH every single day....because YOU ARE!

*If you can't DO GOOD all of the
time . . . . DO GOOD some of
the time and work your way up*

*Blessings in disguise bring something good
to our experience from those moments or
people we wish we hadn't encountered*

The worst of experiences can bring about the best of experiences

There is freedom in true happiness . . .
CHooSe HaPPy!!

There's only power in fear if you allow it.
Fear is nothing more than you giving
your attention to your insecurities

The beautiful thing about today . . . .
is EVERYTHING!!
Find your way to beautiful

If you're not playing nice, don't expect the
kids to play nice. Happiness starts
with you . . . the children will follow

The more you DO GOOD! . . .
the more you FEEL GOOD!

Even when all is lost, there is a spark that
inspires the desire to have again . . . .
and so our new creations begin.
We think . . . . We create

The one who makes excuses prefers to sit and watch the mountain . . . The one with purpose and passion prefers to climb it

Allow your kindness to shine . . . .
you're bound to make someone's day

No matter how many times you drag it up, the past won't change. Pour your energy into where you want to be, not where you've been and leave the past behind

Embrace Different . . . . Different makes the world Interesting

KNOWLEDGE is POWER . . . .
use your POWER for GOOD!!

To truly experience the most wonderful happiness, we must first know how to truly love. LOVE ourselves, LOVE each other and LOVE all that is . . . all the time. Everything else will fall into place

Furnish your life as you would furnish your home . . . Fill it with the stuff that makes you feel good!

If it's weighing you down...
It's holding you back

Dreams are reality waiting to happen . . .
Dare to Launch Your Dreams

You are capable of more than you know.
The only limits are the ones you place upon
yourself. Move beyond your limitations
and let the creative juices flow

You are the only thinker of your thoughts
therefore . . . no-one has the power to
change them but you!

All that you desire is just a thought away

Negative thinking is just YOU *holding* YOU *back from your true potential!*

You will be much happier obtaining the things you desire if you set about making the journey to those things, an enjoyable one

If you think everyone else has all the luck . . . . think again. Those who are perceived as lucky are simply positive thinkers

Love is the key element to all positive emotion

Love holds unlimited power to create

Love is THE most POWERFUL

energy in the universe

The more LOVE you GIVE,

The more LOVE you get

So what are you waiting for????

Get busy LOVIN!!!

Don't just inhale for the sake of breathing. We are surrounded by so many breathtaking reasons to live

It's OK to feed your ego from time to time.
It's called **checking in with yourself
emotionally and physically.**
Love what you see, Enjoy how you feel,
and Embrace who you are!!

The most important one is YOU!!
You can't expect others to love YOU if
YOU don't love YOU!!

As long as there is love to give, there are hearts waiting to receive it ♥♥♥

*Today I am grateful for what
yesterday gave me.
Today I look forward to what tomorrow
is yet to bring*

If I share Love and Kindness with you, chances are . . . you'll be inspired to share it too ♥♥♥

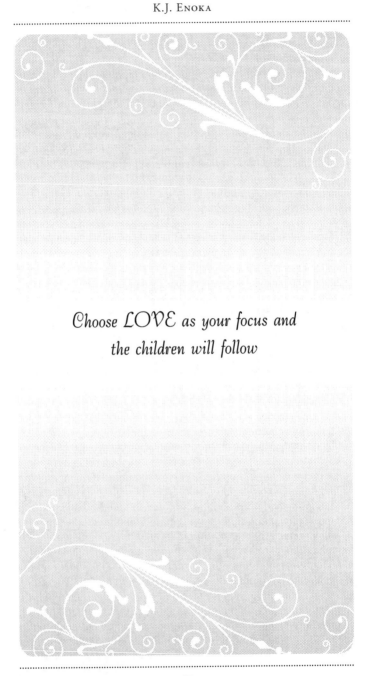

*Choose LOVE as your focus and
the children will follow*

Your so called failures and bad choices
happen for a reason.
The universe has something else
in store for you.
Opportunities abound beyond another door

When you push all negative aside, you position yourself for greater advancement and amazing things start to happen

Time wasted on *HATE* is time
lost on *LOVE*

If you're lovin who you see in the mirror each day, then chances are, those around you will be lovin you too

The thoughts and actions of one is
enough to influence the thoughts
and actions of many.
Create change . . . . make a difference
YOU ARE POWERFUL!!

*Well-being comes to those who allow well-being.
Ill health comes to those who allow ill health.
In other words . . . . if you focus on
how bad you feel, you're resisting the
opportunity to feel better*

Embrace every connection and experience.
No matter how good or bad, there's
a reason for it all

Plant a thought . . . . grow a dream . . . . then watch it come to life

*Appreciation for all things brings more stuff
to make you feel good and when you feel
good, so do those around you . . . .
share the love* ♥

The difference between the **I wish** and
I have way of thinking.
I wish = I hope I get it.
I have = It's already on it's way.
HaPpY CrEaTiNg!!

If you can't find something to smile about,
look forward to, be grateful for,
then you're just not looking hard enough

Even a bad day will eventually get better

If you want the kids to shine, ignite their spirit with lots of good stuff and watch them light up the world

Be grateful for all your experiences. Even the ones that leave a sour taste. It all contributes to the expansion and growth of you

The one you share your life with, should enhance, illuminate and accentuate yours. We should shine brighter because of each other, not in-spite of each other

Our choices, good and bad, give us another perspective on things so we can change our minds, change our paths and create new stuff

You can't expect the flowers to grow
if you keep blocking the sun.
Nourish your soul with love and positive
energy and you too will shine

Push fear aside . . .
it only serves to block the light.
You are the creator of your life.
Trust in the power of your thoughts and
feel safe in knowing that you have the
ability to change the direction your
life takes you

We are all worthy and deserving of great things. Allowing them into our experience is only delayed by what we think and believe

If you have only insults, criticism and unkind words for others, it's because your own self worth is in question and you want others to feel your pain. Rise above it. Positive has more power

SEE the good in others and they'll
SEE the good in you!

Holding grudges creates dis-ease and holds you in a place of unhappiness. Pour all that negative energy into something that makes you feel good

How you think and feel, paves the way for the journey ahead and determines how much fun you have getting there. The beauty of it is, you can change direction and improve the scenery along the way

Often the very thing we are trying to avoid is the very thing that gives us the most wonderful and unexpected experiences and makes the journey all the more exciting.

~ think, create, enjoy ~

The one with the negative outlook will criticise and find fault.
The one with the positive outlook will compliment and see beauty.
What you project is a reflection of YOU

What happens next depends entirely on how YOU think and how YOU react. The choice is always YOURS

Negative thoughts and actions create dis-ease.
Positive thoughts and actions create well-being.
The power of positive is amazing!

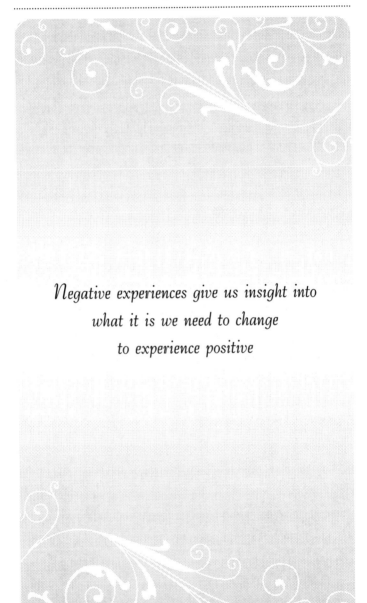

Negative experiences give us insight into what it is we need to change to experience positive

Success is measured not by what you have but, by how it makes you feel

*No one can make you feel anything unless
you allow yourself to feel it*

Love, kindness and positive attitudes are contagious. Just smile and do nice stuff for others and see how many people you infect . . . . enjoy!

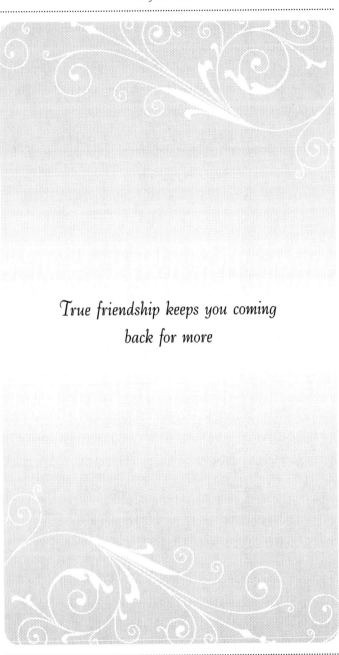

*True friendship keeps you coming
back for more*

You cannot bring about peace by consistently giving your attention to war. The universe will bring more of the same. Peace can only flow when we set a vibrational tone of love and kindness

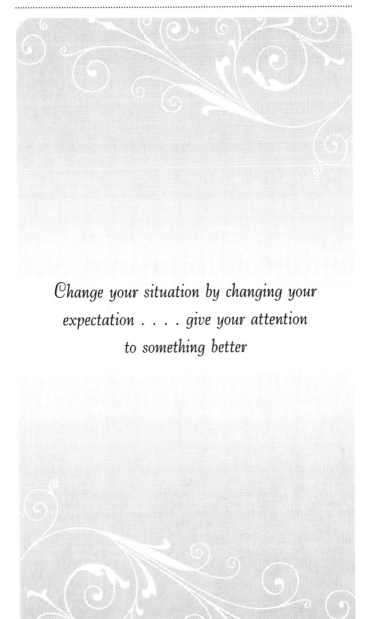

Change your situation by changing your expectation . . . . give your attention to something better

Holding on to grudges and regrets serves no purpose in your life. Your choice to do so imprisons you and keeps you from moving forward. Release them and free yourself from that place

Never look back and wonder what you could have done differently, because what you did then doesn't matter. It's what you do now that will make all the difference!

Don't bring your resentment and anger
with you....it's clouding all the happiness
that's trying to get through
Let it all go!!

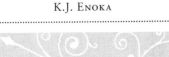

Enthusiasm, passion and an attitude of love will take you to amazing places!

Allow yourself to Love and be loved. When you truly love who you are, you resonate with the universe and attract the most wonderful people and experiences

Believe in YOU . . . . YOU are beautiful

The only one who can take credit for the things that happen to YOU, for YOU, within YOU . . . is YOU.
You think it . . . . you create it!

An eye for an eye attitude will NEVER
EVER solve the problem but it will
ALWAYS ALWAYS create more!
Don't take action with a heart full of
hate . . . you'll never win!

You don't get good at anything unless you try. Experience comes from experience

Fill your life with the people and things
that influence you in a positive way

*I look back on the negative experiences and
say . . . . Thank you Universe . . .
for pointing me in another direction*

The sooner you bring joy and love to all that you do . . . the quicker you reach your happy place

Let the past go and everything will flow

Age gracefully but, age gratefully. Old age simply means Mother Nature has seen fit to extend your visit here on earth. Love the skin you're in and enjoy the rest of your life

*If you don't like the story so far, change it.
You're the author of your life . . . you get
to tell a different story, a better story*

Our experiences are not governed by luck...
but by thought.
Good thoughts = good stuff
Bad thoughts = bad stuff

Love em or hate em, the people in your life
(past and present) have come to you
for a reason and that is why,
you are where you are today.
And the ones who are yet to pass through,
will contribute to where you'll be tomorrow

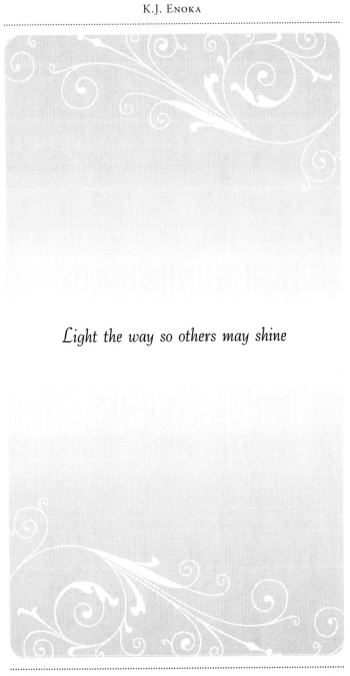

Light the way so others may shine

A life in perfect balance is blessed
with all that is positive and good

The ones that want you in their lives will make room for you when the time is right, just as you will make room for them

If you keep going to that place you don't like, you're gonna keep getting the same result. There's another choice just over there you might like to try.
Choose better . . . feel better

Be kind and love a lot . . . .
it's the right thing to do

Let go and embrace change....the next episode of your journey is about to begin